INSPIRE
HAIR FASHION FOR SALON CLIENTS

Pivot Point International HAIR: Joakim Roos MAKE-UP: Dino PHOTO: Mike van den Toorn/Tina Rayyan

INSPIRE
HAIR FASHION FOR SALON CLIENTS

Featuring COLOR

Table of Contents Volume 67

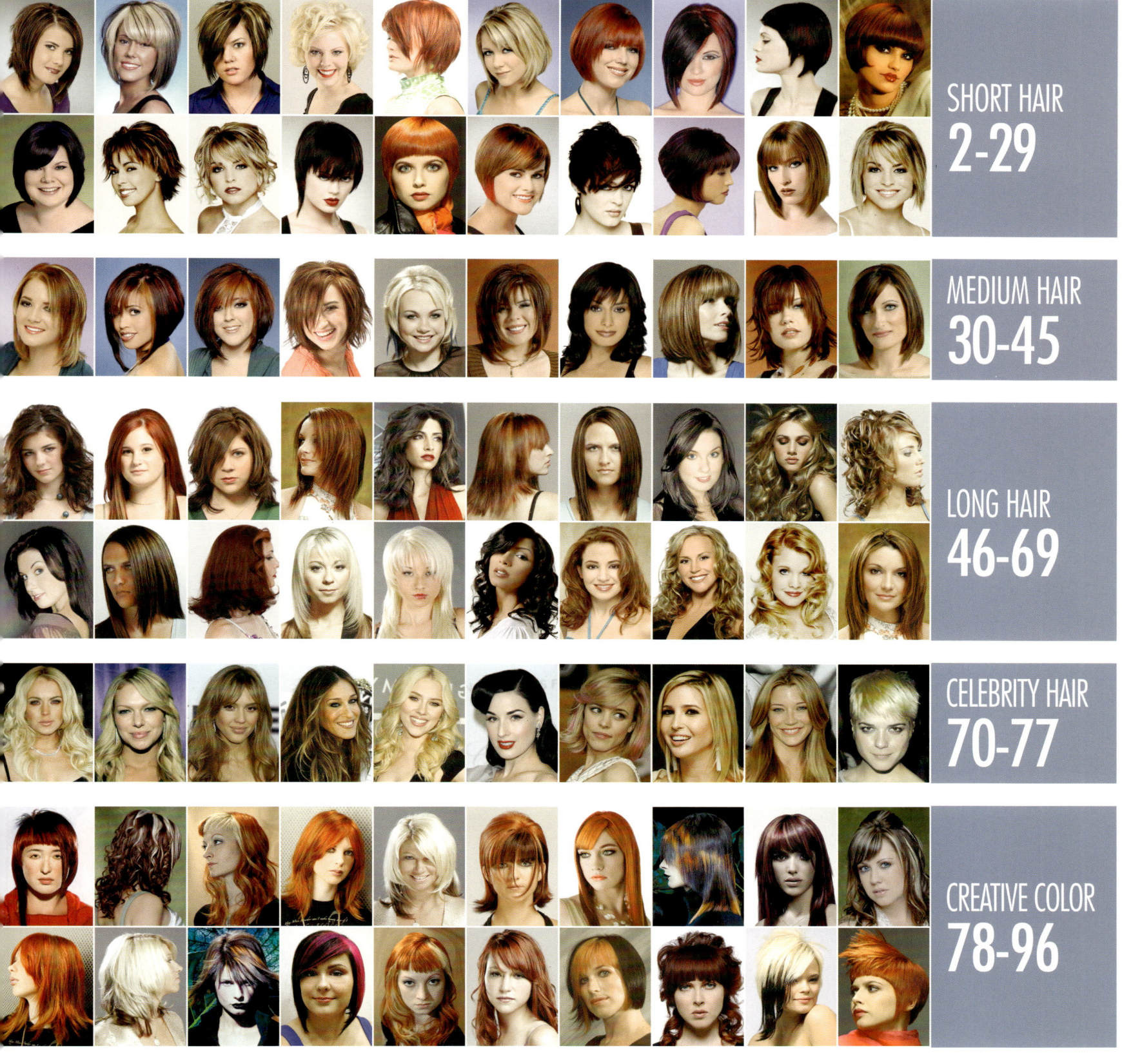

SHORT HAIR 2-29

MEDIUM HAIR 30-45

LONG HAIR 46-69

CELEBRITY HAIR 70-77

CREATIVE COLOR 78-96

Liza Espinoza-Achurra Designs
HAIR: Liza Espinoza-Achurra
MAKEUP: Jill Gosser
PHOTO: Steven Ledell

SHORT HAIR

Vincent Michael Salon
HAIR: Darren Reyes
MAKEUP: Jaime Queenin
PHOTO: Taggart Winterhalter
for Purely Visual

Michael Angelo Salon & Spa
HAIR: Jamie Savage
COLOR: Jamie Savage
MAKEUP: Jenna Thompson
PHOTO: Michael Razzo

SHORT HAIR

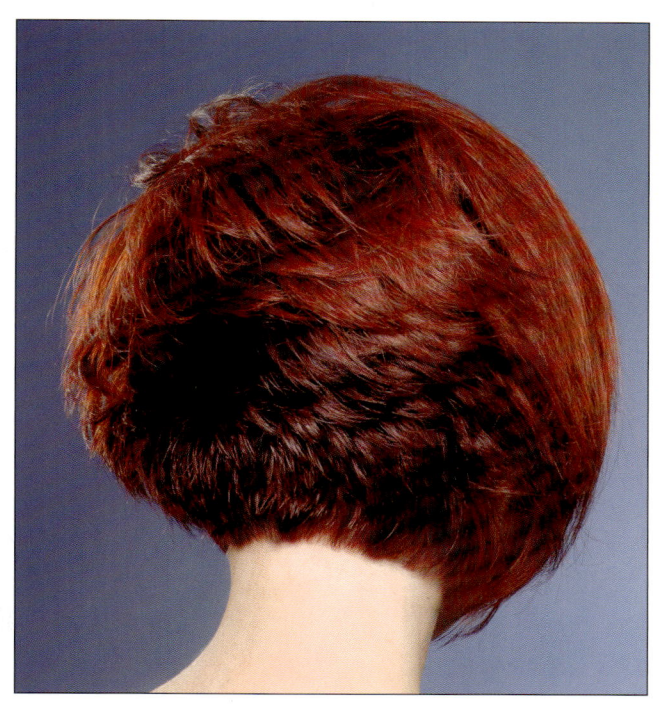

Carter T. Lund and Associates
HAIR: Carter T. Lund
MAKEUP: Sara Wayne & Jaime Queenin
PHOTO: Taggart Winterhalter for Purely Visual

Siggers Hairdressers Salon-Tucker, GA
HAIR: Mary Jac Beavers
COLOR: Lea Baselici
MAKEUP: Suni Tucker
PHOTO: Scott Bryant
Art Direction by Larry Oskin & The Marketing Solutions Team

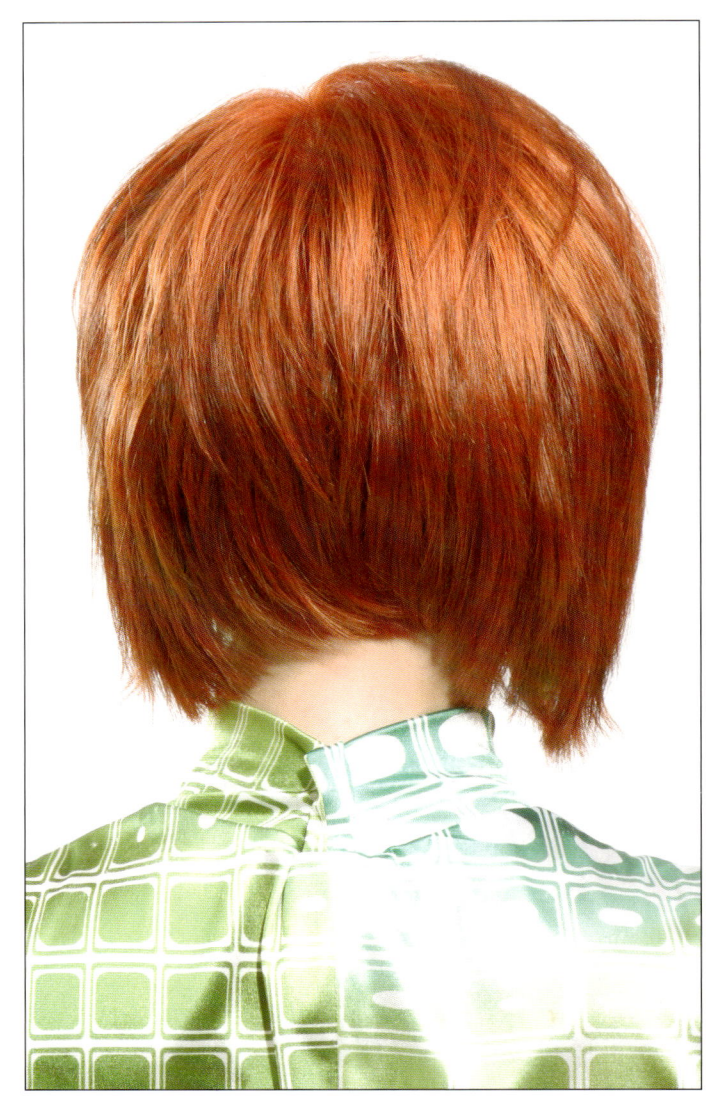

SHORT HAIR

Hair Benders Internationalé
HAIR: Hair Benders Design Team
COLOR: Hair Benders Design Team
MAKEUP: Darin Wright
PHOTO: Scott Bryant
Art Direction by Larry Oskin & The Marketing Solutions Team

Planet Salon-Lexington, KY
HAIR: Noah Taylor
MAKEUP: Noah Taylor
PHOTO: Jeff Rogers

Anazao Salon
HAIR: Jauton Bender
MAKEUP: Jauton Bender
PHOTO: Robert B. Pendley

Infrashine
HAIR: Steve and Cyndi Lehman for InfraShine
MAKEUP: Jaime Queenin
PHOTO: Taggart Winterhalter for Purely Visual

Vincent Michael Salon
HAIR: Christina Voge
MAKEUP: Sara Wayne
PHOTO: Taggart Winterhalter for Purely Visual

SHORT HAIR

Kadus USA
HAIR: Jessee Skittrall
MAKEUP: Jaime Queenin
PHOTO: Taggart Winterhalter
for Purely Visual

Kadus USA
HAIR: Jessee Skittrall
MAKEUP: Jaime Queenin
PHOTO: Taggart Winterhalter
for Purely Visual

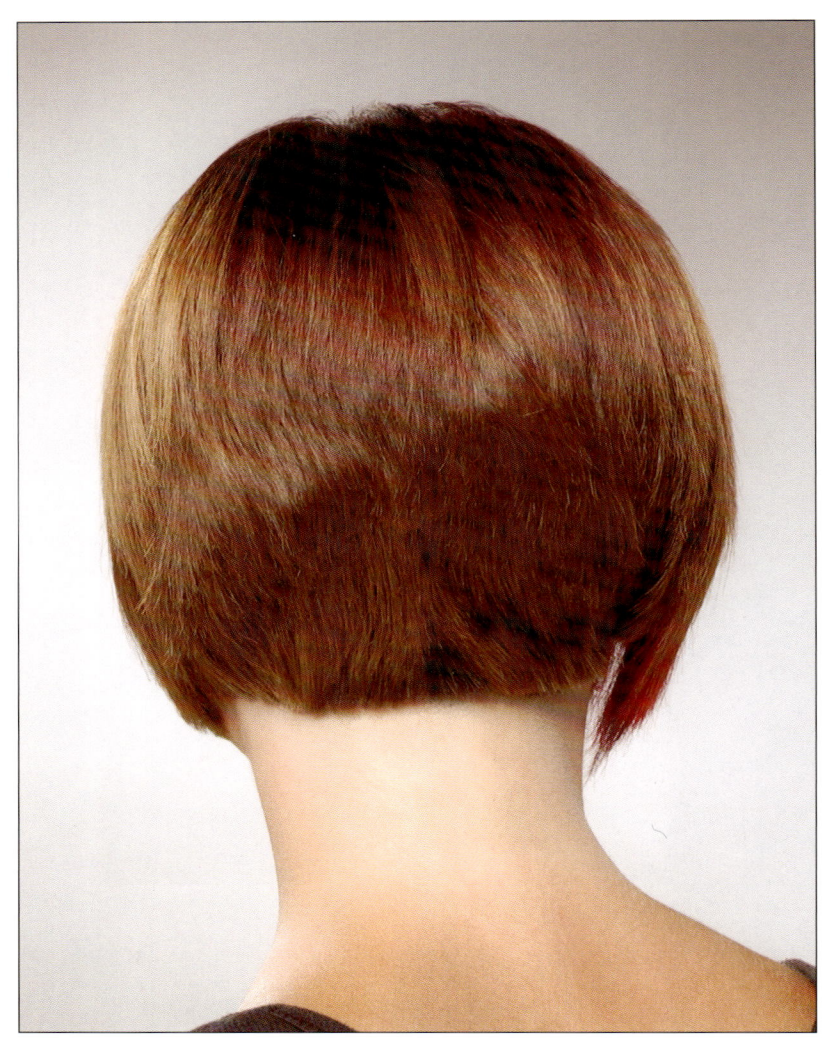

Vincent Michael Salon
HAIR: Patrick Ryan
MAKEUP: Sara Wayne
PHOTO: Taggart Winterhalter
for Purely Visual

Sempre Bellezza
HAIR: Celeste J. Aldrete
MAKEUP: Jaime Queenin
PHOTO: Taggart Winterhalter for Purely Visual

Intercoiffure
HAIR: Gaëlle
MAKEUP: Sébastian
PHOTO: Yannick

SHORT HAIR

Salon Serene
HAIR: Laura Barsotti
MAKEUP: Laura Barsotti
PHOTO: Jean Sweet

**PON International
Anaheim Hills, CA**
HAIR: Steven Villa
MAKEUP: Jaime Queenin
PHOTO: Taggart Winterhalter
for Purely Visual

SHORT HAIR

Crème Colour Lounge
HAIR: Valerie Braden
MAKEUP: Sara Wayne
PHOTO: Taggart Winterhalter
for Purely Visual

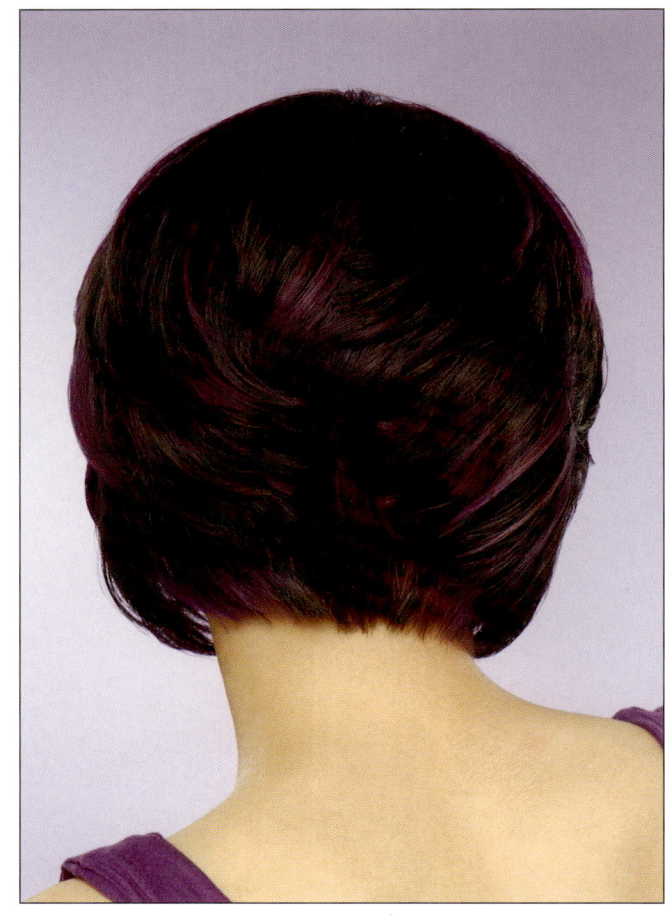

Salon Dé Dawn
HAIR: Dawn Orlow Townsend
MAKEUP: Jaime Queenin
PHOTO: Taggart Winterhalter
for Purely Visual

SHORT HAIR

Vincent Michael Salon
HAIR: Vincent Michael for ENJOY
MAKEUP: Sara Wayne
PHOTO: Taggart Winterhalter for Purely Visual

Tangles Hair Lounge
HAIR: Kelly Dobbert
MAKEUP: Jaime Queenin
PHOTO: Taggart Winterhalter for Purely Visual

19

Stray Cuts
HAIR: Brandon Hyman
MAKEUP: Sara Wayne
PHOTO: Taggart Winterhalter for Purely Visual

Sempre Bellezza
HAIR: Daniella DelFante
MAKEUP: Sara Wayne
PHOTO: Taggart Winterhalter for Purely Visual

Infrashine
HAIR: Steve and Cyndi Lehman for InfraShine
MAKEUP: Jaime Queenin
PHOTO: Taggart Winterhalter for Purely Visual

SHORT HAIR

ENJOY Hair Care
HAIR: Vincent Michael
COLOR: Vincent Michael
MAKEUP: Jaime Queenin
PHOTO: Taggart Winterhalter
for Purely Visual

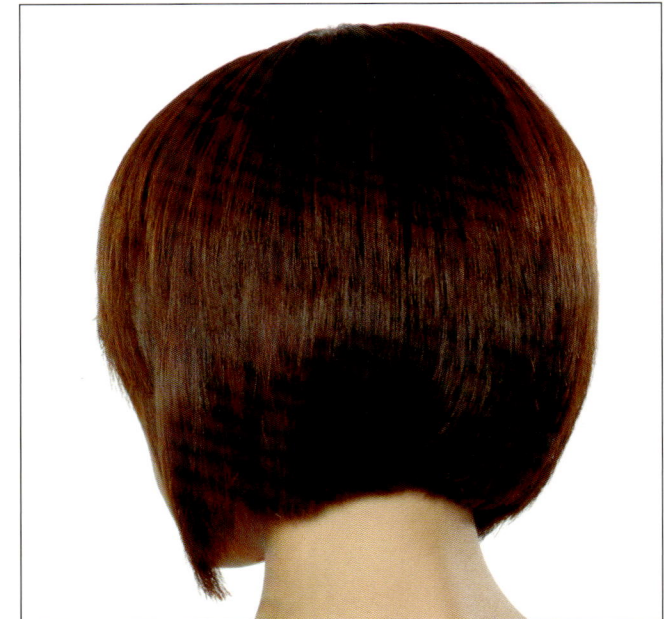

SHORT HAIR

élon Salon
HAIR: Nina Garry
COLOR: Nina Garry
MAKEUP: Nina Garry
PHOTO: Scott Bryant
Art Direction by Larry Oskin
& The Marketing
Solutions Team

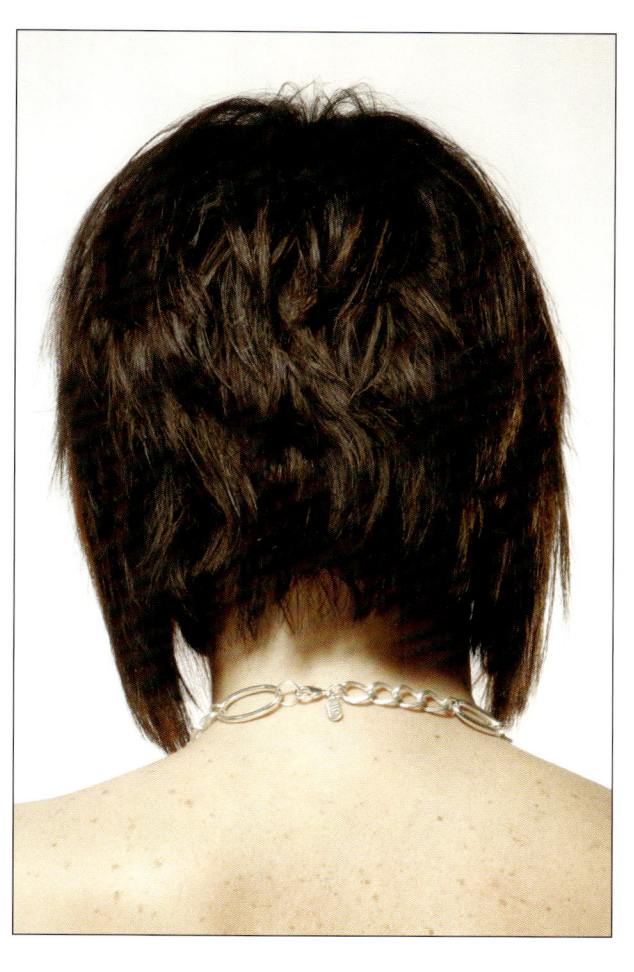

ENJOY Hair Care
HAIR: Nick Flier
COLOR: Pat Drake
MAKEUP: Jaime Queenin
PHOTO: Taggart Winterhalter
for Purely Visual

SHORT HAIR

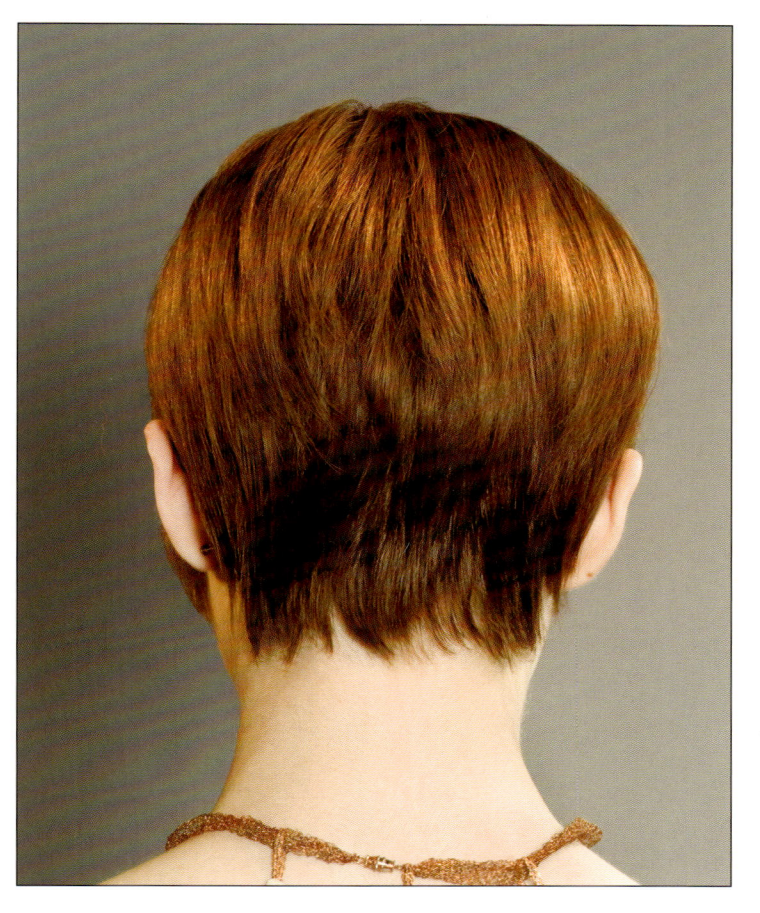

Salon Serene
HAIR: Laura Barsotti
MAKEUP: Laura Barsotti
PHOTO: Jean Sweet

Salon Serene
HAIR: Laura Barsotti
MAKEUP: Jean Sweet
PHOTO: Jean Sweet

Brittany's Spa Salon
HAIR: Brittany Molina
COLOR: Brittany Molina
MAKEUP: Brittany Molina
PHOTO: Scott Bryant
Art Direction by
Larry Oskin &
The Marketing
Solutions Team

Infrashine
HAIR: Steve and Cyndi Lehman for InfraShine
MAKEUP: Jaime Queenin
PHOTO: Taggart Winterhalter for Purely Visual

Eveline Charles Salons & Spas
HAIR: Cyndi Issac
MAKEUP: Cheryl Jones
PHOTO: Darren Greenwood

Fantastic Sams
HAIR: Julie Schafer
MAKEUP: Jaime Queenin
PHOTO: Taggart Winterhalter
for Purely Visual

SHORT HAIR

**PON International-
Anaheim Hills, CA**
HAIR: Sara Wayne
MAKEUP: Sara Wayne
PHOTO: Taggart Winterhalter
for Purely Visual

**PON International-
Anaheim Hills, CA**
HAIR: Todd Snow
MAKEUP: Sara Wayne
PHOTO: Taggart Winterhalter
for Purely Visual

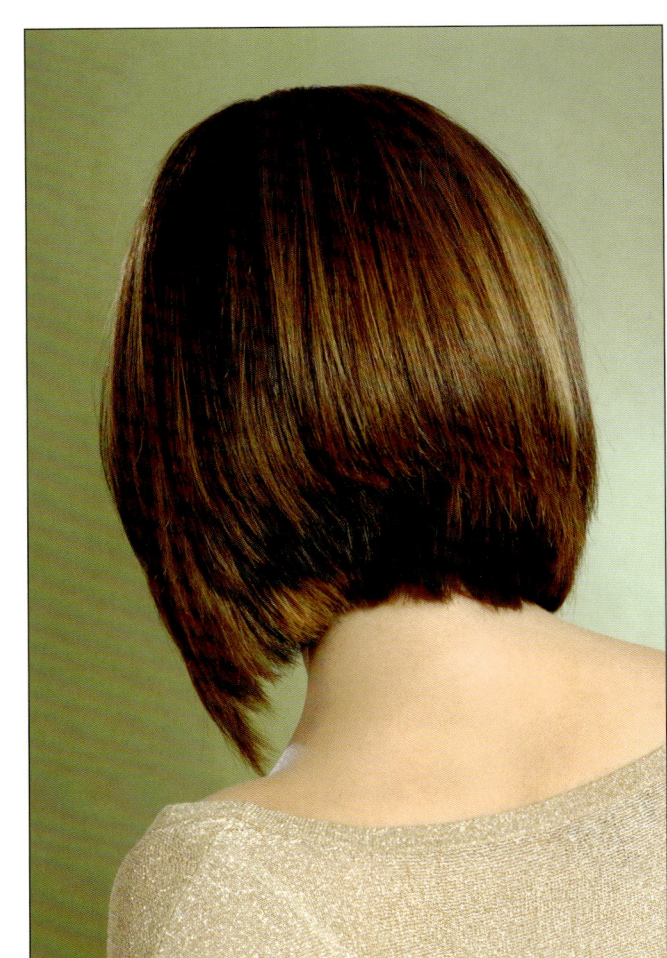

Alexander's Grand Salon & Spa
HAIR: Denise Gudino
MAKEUP: Katrina Halliwell
PHOTO: Taggart Winterhalter
for Purely Visual

Alexander's Grand Salon & Spa
HAIR: Michelle Alexander
MAKEUP: Katrina Halliwell
PHOTO: Taggart Winterhalter
for Purely Visual

MEDIUM HAIR

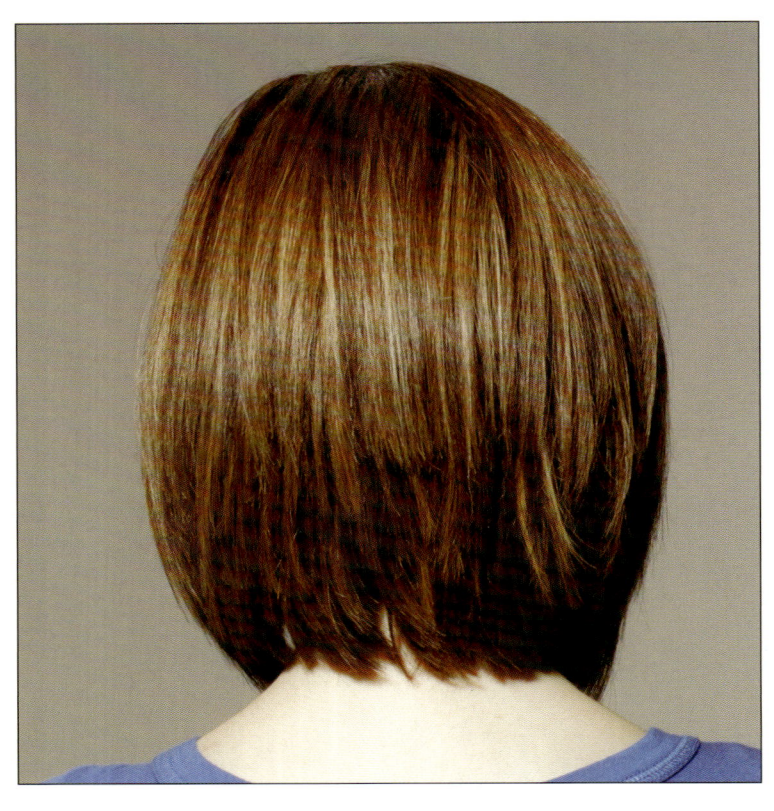

élon Salon
HAIR: Emily Bruce
COLOR: Emily Bruce
MAKEUP: Lili Casanova
PHOTO: Scott Bryant
Art Direction by Larry Oskin &
The Marketing Solutions Team

ENJOY Hair Care
HAIR: Donny Anderson
COLOR: Donny Anderson
MAKEUP: Jaime Queenin
PHOTO: Taggart Winterhalter
for Purely Visual

MEDIUM HAIR

33

Alexander's Grand Salon & Spa
HAIR: Yesenia Quebrado
MAKEUP: Merle Fye
PHOTO: Taggart Winterhalter
for Purely Visual

MEDIUM HAIR

élon Salon
HAIR: Ray Brookshire
COLOR: Ray Brookshire
HAIR EXTENSION: Ray Brookshire
MAKEUP: Lili Casanova
PHOTO: Scott Bryant
Art Direction by Larry Oskin &
The Marketing Solutions Team

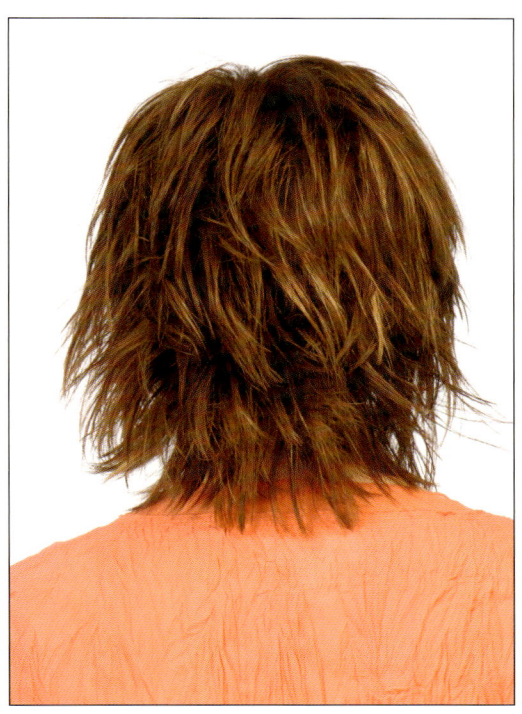

élon Salon
HAIR: Deborah Westbrook
COLOR: Deborah Westbrook
MAKEUP: Fawn/Mac
PHOTO: Scott Bryant
Art Direction by Larry Oskin &
The Marketing Solutions Team

Carter T. Lund and Associates
HAIR: Carter T. Lund
MAKEUP: Sara Wayne & Jaime Queenin
PHOTO: Taggart Winterhalter
for Purely Visual

Carter T. Lund and Associates
HAIR: Carter T. Lund
MAKEUP: Sara Wayne & Jaime Queenin
PHOTO: Taggart Winterhalter
for Purely Visual

Salon Dé Dawn
HAIR: Dawn Orlow Townsend
MAKEUP: Sara Wayne
PHOTO: Taggart Winterhalter for Purely Visual

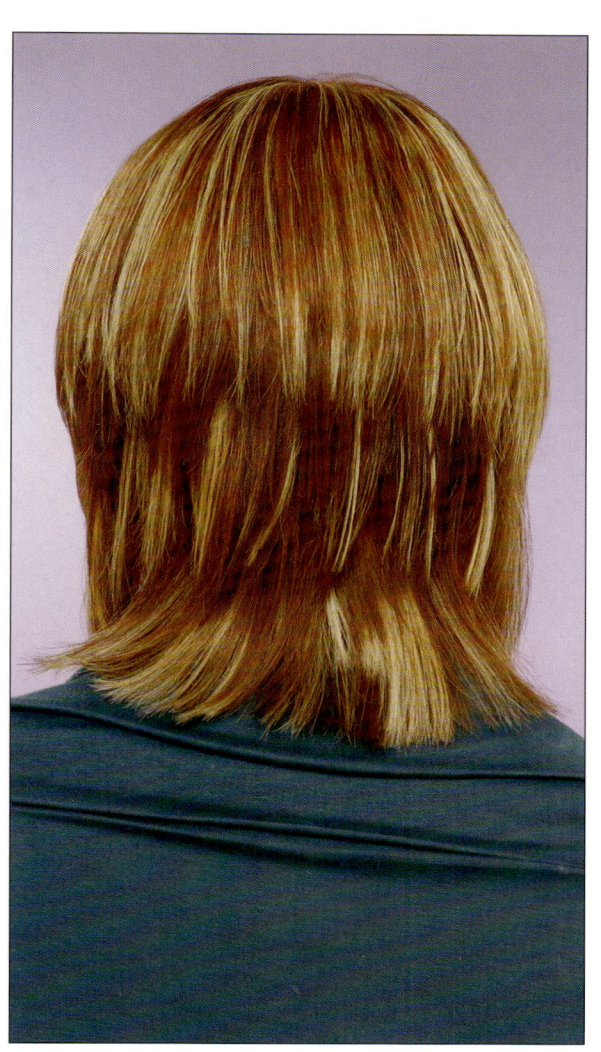

MEDIUM HAIR

Salon Serene
HAIR: Laura Barsotti
MAKEUP: Jean Sweet
PHOTO: Jean Sweet

MEDIUM HAIR

élon Salon
HAIR: Nina Garry
COLOR: Nina Garry
MAKEUP: Nina Garry
PHOTO: Scott Bryant
Art Direction by Larry Oskin &
The Marketing Solutions Team

Cosmos Hair and Day Spa
HAIR: Sandra Lee Barbetta
MAKEUP: Jaime Queenin
PHOTO: Taggart Winterhalter
for Purely Visual

Advanced College of Cosmetology
HAIR: Advanced College
of Cosmetology
MAKEUP: Advanced College
of Cosmetology
PHOTO: Doug Raflik

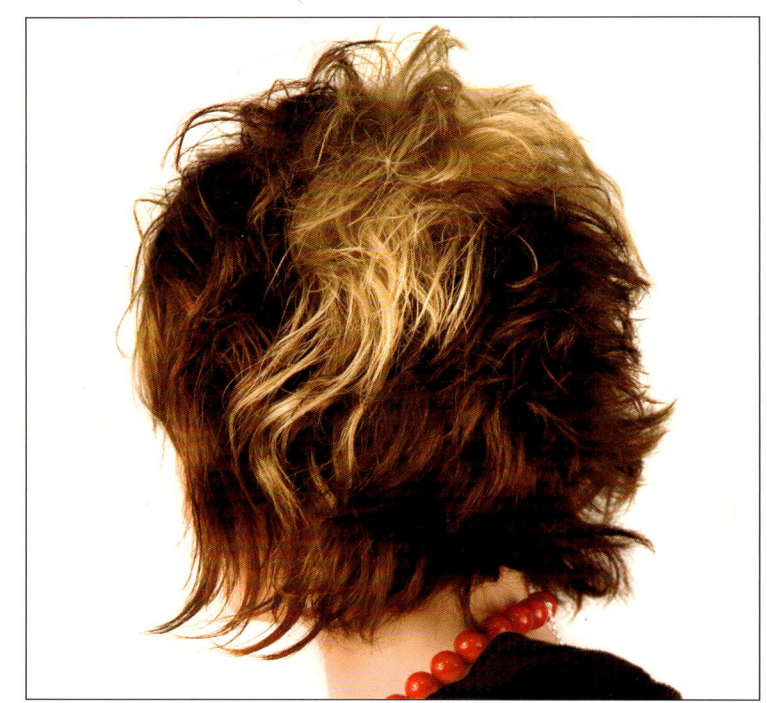

Fantastic Sams
HAIR: Man San Yong
MAKEUP: Jaime Queenin
PHOTO: Taggart Winterhalter for Purely Visual

MEDIUM HAIR

Doyle Designed Salon
HAIR: Doyle Sims
MAKEUP: Doyle Sims
PHOTO: Deborah Zaniolo

Fantastic Sams
HAIR: Rosalia Guana
MAKEUP: Jaime Queenin
PHOTO: Taggart Winterhalter
for Purely Visual

Fantastic Sams
HAIR: Shelley Whitaker
MAKEUP: Jaime Queenin
PHOTO: Taggart Winterhalter
for Purely Visual

MEDIUM HAIR

Art of Hair Salon
HAIR: Nicole Martin
MAKEUP: Jaime Queenin
PHOTO: Taggart Winterhalter
for Purely Visual

PON International-Anaheim Hills, CA
HAIR: Mandi Bevando
MAKEUP: Sara Wayne
PHOTO: Taggart Winterhalter
for Purely Visual

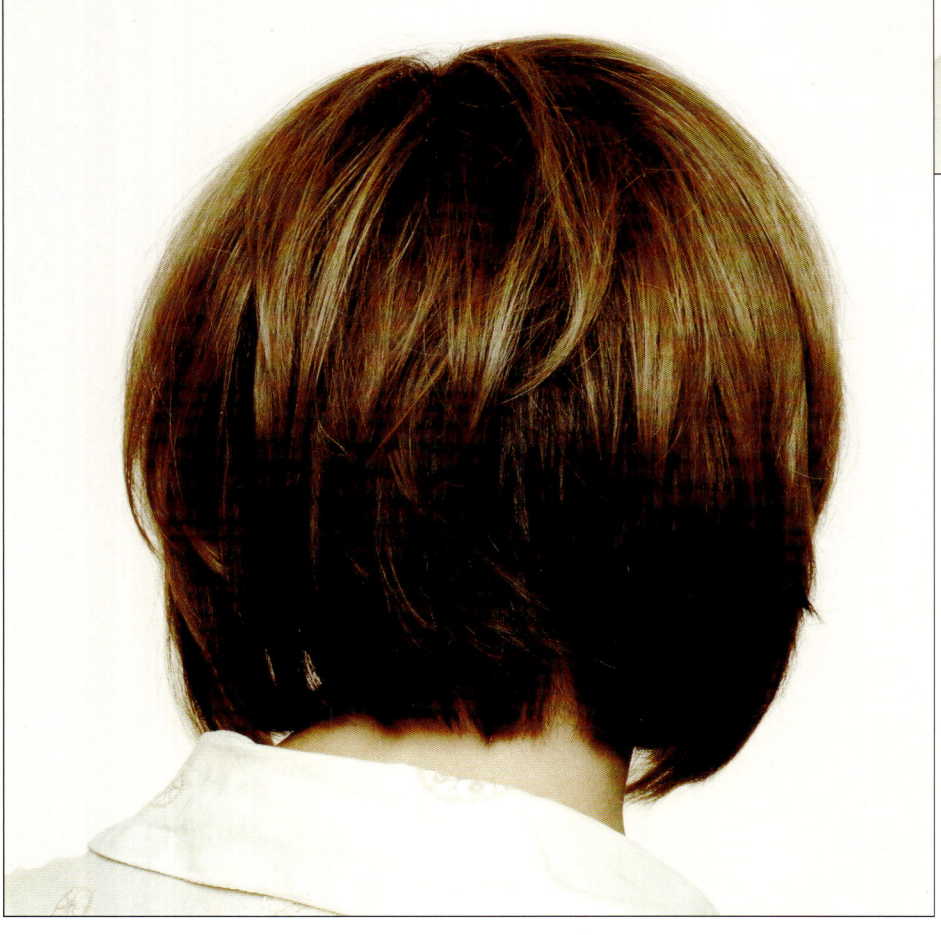

MEDIUM HAIR

PON International-Anaheim Hills, CA
HAIR: Kathy Reed
MAKEUP: Jaime Queenin
PHOTO: Taggart Winterhalter
for Purely Visual

Avant Gard Hair Salon
HAIR: Amber Lyons
COLOR: Amber Lyons
MAKEUP: Amber Lyons
PHOTO: Scott Bryant
Art Direction by Larry Oskin &
The Marketing Solutions Team

Mitchell's Salons & Day Spas
HAIR: Vivian Moore
MAKEUP: Lydia Brock
PHOTO: Annette McCall

LONG HAIR

Mina's Studio and Spa
HAIR: Crystal Mays-Balster
MAKEUP: Angela Caparo
PHOTO: Jan Balster

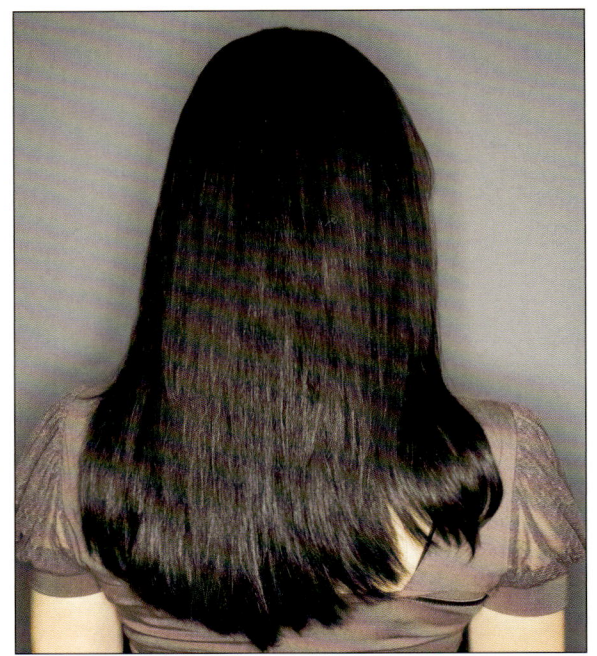

Avant Gard Hair Salon
HAIR: A.J. Williams
COLOR: A.J. Williams
MAKEUP: Lacey Walker
PHOTO: Scott Bryant
Art Direction by Larry Oskin &
The Marketing Solutions Team

LONG HAIR

Art of Hair
HAIR: Jeffery John
MAKEUP: Sara Wayne
PHOTO: Taggart Winterhalter
for Purely Visual

Diadema Hair Fashion
HAIR: Diadema
MAKEUP: 20100Milano
PHOTO: Stefano Bidini

LONG HAIR

Kathy Adams Salon
HAIR: Kathy Adams Salon Team
MAKEUP: Kathy Adams Salon Team
PHOTO: Tom Carson Photography

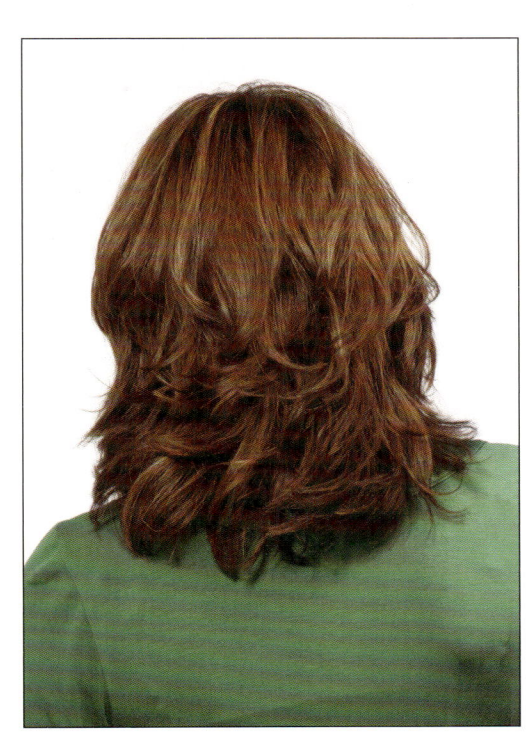

élon Salon
HAIR: Andrea Lopez
COLOR: Andrea Lopez
MAKEUP: Nico
PHOTO: Scott Bryant
Art Direction by Larry Oskin & The Marketing Solutions Team

Graham Webb International Academy of Hair-Arlington, VA
HAIR: Alisha Chenery
COLOR: Alisha Chenery
MAKEUP: Alisha Chenery
PHOTO: Scott Bryant
Art Direction by Larry Oskin &
The Marketing Solutions Team

Hair Benders Internationalé-Chattanooga, TN
HAIR: Hair Benders Design Team
COLOR: Hair Benders Design Team
MAKEUP: Darin Wright
PHOTO: Scott Bryant
Art Direction by Larry Oskin &
The Marketing Solutions Team

LONG HAIR

Infrashine
HAIR: Steve and Cyndi Lehman for InfraShine
MAKEUP: Jaime Queenin
PHOTO: Taggart Winterhalter for Purely Visual

CinderellaHair
HAIR: Jessee Skittrall
EXTENSIONS: Cindy Stillwagon
MAKEUP: Jaime Queenin
PHOTO: Taggart Winterhalter
for Purely Visual

PON International-Anaheim Hills, CA
HAIR: Kathy Reed
MAKEUP: Sara Wayne
PHOTO: Taggart Winterhalter
for Purely Visual

Edie's Styling Center
HAIR: Jessica Butler
COLOR: Jessica Butler
MAKEUP: Lili Casanova
PHOTO: Scott Bryant
Art Direction by
Larry Oskin
& The Marketing
Solutions Team

LONG HAIR

57

CinderellaHair
HAIR: Cindy Stillwagon,
Judee Lunman, Jessee Skittrall
MAKEUP: Jaime Queenin
PHOTO: Taggart Winterhalter
for Purely Visual

CinderellaHair
HAIR: Maggie DeSanchis,
Jessee Skittrall
MAKEUP: Jaime Queenin
PHOTO: Taggart Winterhalter
for Purely Visual

CinderellaHair
HAIR: Jessee Skittrall
EXTENSIONS: Cindy Stillwagon
MAKEUP: Jaime Queenin
PHOTO: Taggart Winterhalter
for Purely Visual

CinderellaHair
HAIR: Jessee Skittrall
EXTENSIONS: Cindy Stillwagon
MAKEUP: Jaime Queenin
PHOTO: Taggart Winterhalter
for Purely Visual

LONG HAIR

élon Salon
HAIR: Kelly Newman
COLOR: Deborah Westbrook
MAKEUP: Kelley Newman
PHOTO: Scott Bryant
Art Direction by Larry Oskin
& The Marketing Solutions Team

élon Salon
HAIR: Lisa Jordan
COLOR: Lisa Jordan
MAKEUP: Fawn/Mac
PHOTO: Scott Bryant
Art Direction by
Larry Oskin
& The Marketing
Solutions Team

Goldwell Colorance Team
HAIR: Goldwell Colorance Team
MAKEUP: Goldwell Colorance Team
PHOTO: Goldwell Colorance Team

LONG HAIR

élon Salon
HAIR: Tara Griffin
COLOR: Tara Griffin
MAKEUP: Fawn/Mac
PHOTO: Scott Bryant
Art Direction by
Larry Oskin
& The Marketing
Solutions Team

Alexander's Grand Salon & Spa
HAIR: Angelica Cosoi
MAKEUP: Kari Hoyt
PHOTO: Taggart Winterhalter for Purely Visual

LONG HAIR

Anazao Salon
HAIR: Jauton Bender
MAKEUP: Jauton Bender
PHOTO: Robert B. Pendley

HAIR: Angela Smith
MAKEUP: Mickey Guedea
PHOTO: Eliisa Maki

LONG HAIR

Edie's Styling Center
HAIR: Albree Strouse
COLOR: Albree Strouse
MAKEUP: Lili Casanova
PHOTO: Scott Bryant
Art Direction by
Larry Oskin &
The Marketing
Solutions Team

Edie's Styling Center
HAIR: Edie Noppenberger
COLOR: Edie Noppenberger
MAKEUP: Lili Casanova
PHOTO: Scott Bryant
Art Direction by Larry Oskin & The Marketing Solutions Team

LONG HAIR

Creative Design A.T.C.
HAIR: Ron Barnes
MAKEUP: Katie Wieland
PHOTO: Brian Morgan

Edie's Styling Center
HAIR: Edie Noppenberger
COLOR: Edie Noppenberger
MAKEUP: Allbree Strouse
PHOTO: Scott Bryant
Art Direction by Larry Oskin & The Marketing Solutions Team

Fantastic Sams
HAIR: Linda Herrera
MAKEUP: Jaime Queenin
PHOTO: Taggart Winterhalter
for Purely Visual

Fantastic Sams
HAIR: Hong (Jessica) Nguyen
MAKEUP: Jaime Queenin
PHOTO: Taggart Winterhalter
for Purely Visual

London Salon and Spa
HAIR: Beth Sternberg
MAKEUP: Bruce London
PHOTO: Ed Flores

LONG HAIR

Selma Blair
PHOTO: Anthony Harvey/WireImage

Ivanka Trump
PHOTO: Amy Sussman/Getty Images

Laura Prepon
PHOTO: Jean-Paul Aussenard
WireImage

Rachel McAdams
PHOTO: Frank Micelotta/Getty Images

Dita Von Teese
PHOTO: Michael Tran/FilmMagic

CELEBRITY HAIR

Scarlett Johansson
PHOTO: KMazur/WireImage

Scarlett Johansson
PHOTO: Evan Agostini/Getty Images

Scarlett Johansson
PHOTO: Pascal Le Segretain/Getty Images

Jessica Alba
PHOTO: Gregg DeGuire/WireImage

Laura Prepon
PHOTO: KMazur/WireImage

Lindsay Lohan
PHOTO: Michael Buckner/
Getty Images

Hayden Panettiere
PHOTO: Jason LaVeris
FilmMagic

CELEBRITY HAIR

Pink
PHOTO: Jon Kopaloff/FilmMagic

Pink
PHOTO: Peter Kramer/Getty Images

Pink
PHOTO: Barry King/WireImage

Lily Allen
PHOTO: Nick Harvey/WireImage

CELEBRITY HAIR

Brenda Strong
PHOTO: Jon Kopaloff/FilmMagic

Debra Messing
PHOTO: Steve Granitz/WireImage

Jamie Pressly
PHOTO: Byron Gamarro/Getty Images

Madonna
PHOTO: Kevin Mazur/WireImage

Emma Griffiths
PHOTO: Eamonn McCormack/ WireImage

Susie Castillo
PHOTO: Michael Loccisano/ FilmMagic

Ashlee Simpson
PHOTO: Jon Kopaloff/ FilmMagic

Sarah Roeme
PHOTO: Jon Kopaloff/ FilmMagic

Jenna Elfman
PHOTO: Jon Kopaloff/FilmMagic

Neve Campbell
PHOTO: Jason Merritt/FilmMagic

Sarah Jessica Parker
PHOTO: Jeffery Mayer/WireImage

Bonnie Somerville
PHOTO: Jon Kopaloff/FilmMagic

CELEBRITY HAIR

Fantastic Sams
HAIR: Shelly Whitaker
PHOTO: Taggart Winterhalter for Purely Visual

Goldwell
HAIR: Trend Zoom 08: The Contra Collection
PHOTO: Goldwell

CREATIVE COLOR

Pivot Point International
HAIR: Simone Muterle, Pivot Point Italy
MAKEUP: Dino
PHOTO: Mike van den Toom/David Placek

Robert Allen Salon
HAIR: David Tinoco
MAKEUP: David Stephens Cosmetics
PHOTO: Boyer Images LLC

CREATIVE COLOR

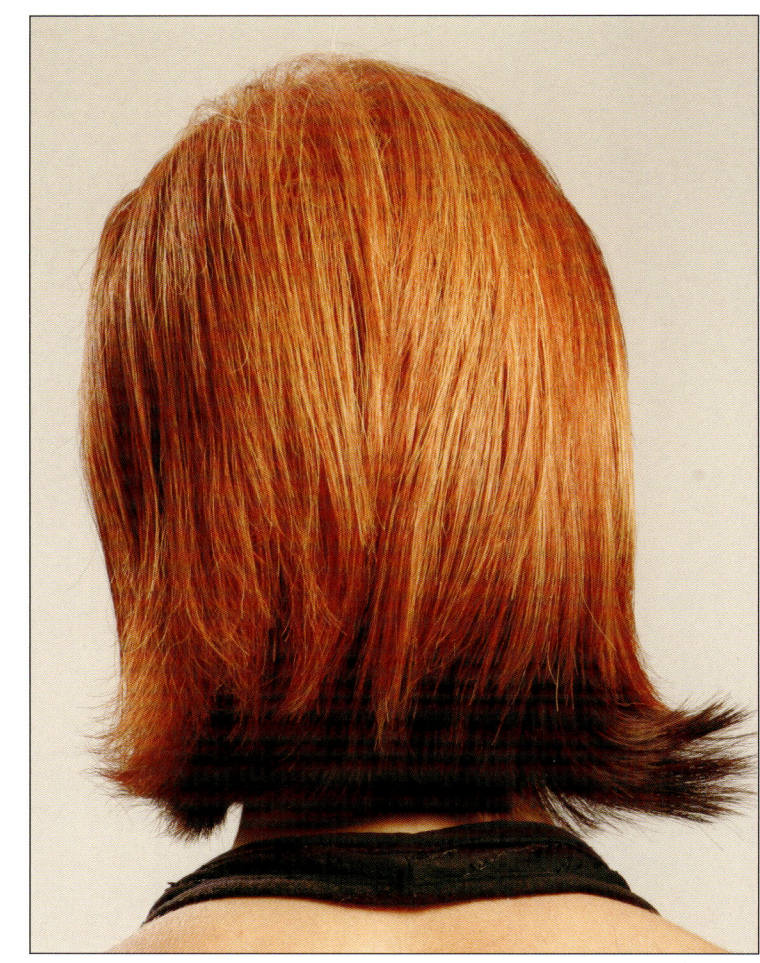

John Amico Haircare & Jalyd Haircolor
HAIR: Yenz & Reinout Von Tilborg
COLOR: Yenz & Reinout Von Tilborg
MAKEUP: Yenz & Reinout Von Tilborg
PHOTO: Scott Bryant
Art Direction by Larry Oskin
& The Marketing Solutions Team

CREATIVE COLOR

Avant Gard Hair Salon
HAIR: Emily Laws
COLOR: Emily Laws
MAKEUP: Avant Gard Hair Salon Team
PHOTO: Scott Bryant
Art Direction by Larry Oskin
& The Marketing Solutions Team

Kathy Adams Salon
HAIR: Kathy Adams Salon Team
MAKEUP: Kathy Adams Salon Team
PHOTO: Tom Carson Photography

Blue Chair Salon
HAIR: Paul Kovacevic
MAKEUP: Paul Kovacevic
PHOTO: Blue Chair Salon

CREATIVE COLOR

Fantastic Sams
HAIR: Shelly Whitaker
PHOTO: Taggart Winterhalter
for Purely Visual

Pivot Point International Germany
HAIR: Vic Piccolotto-Pivot Point Australia
MAKEUP: Dino
PHOTO: Mike van den Toorn/Tina Rayyan

CREATIVE COLOR

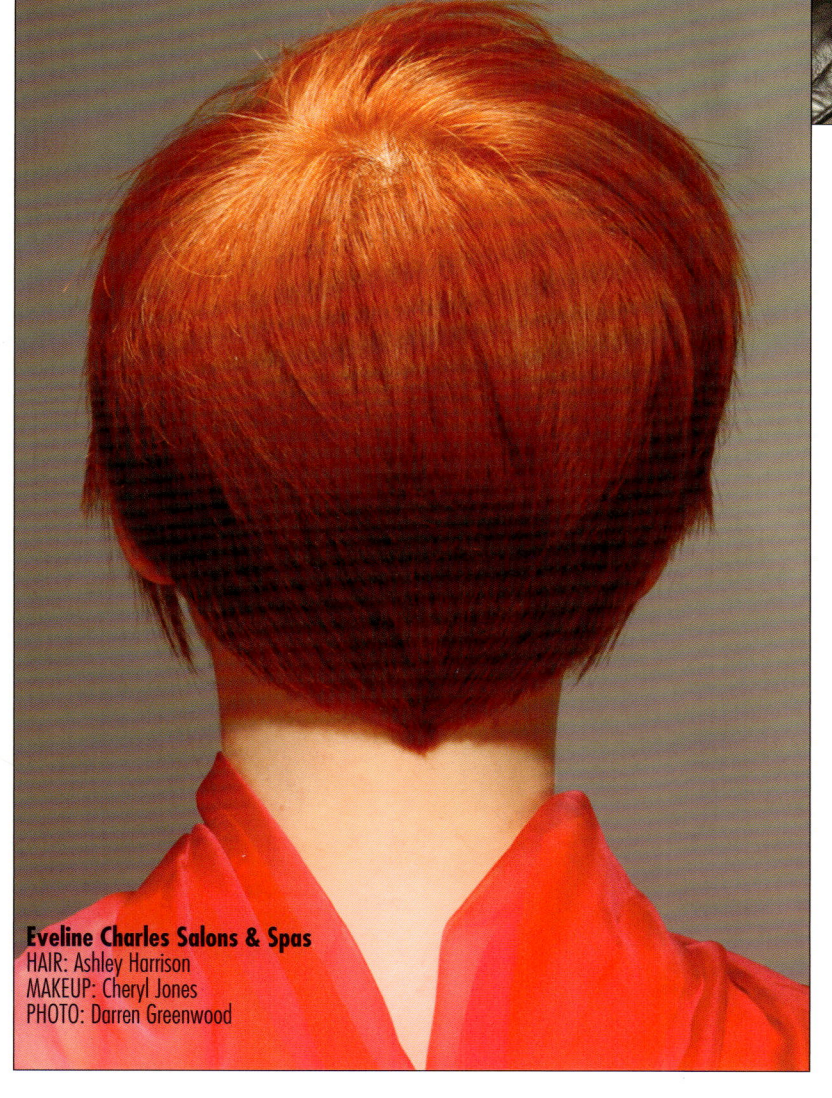

Eveline Charles Salons & Spas
HAIR: Ashley Harrison
MAKEUP: Cheryl Jones
PHOTO: Darren Greenwood

Fantastic Sams
HAIR: Ryan Digregorio
MAKEUP: Jaime Queenin
PHOTO: Taggart Winterhalter
for Purely Visual

Indiana's Premier Hair Academy
HAIR: Josef Settle
COLOR: Josef Settle
MAKEUP: Indiana's Premier Hair Academy Team
PHOTO: Scott Bryant
Art Direction by Larry Oskin & The Marketing Solutions Team

CREATIVE COLOR

Rubia Salon & Spa
HAIR: Renee Russo
MAKEUP: Lindsey Provence
PHOTO: Jim Laatsch

Beauty First
HAIR: Rachel Wertz
MAKEUP: Amanda Knight
PHOTO: Amanda Knight

Avant Gard Hair Salon
HAIR: Josef Settle
COLOR: Josef Settle
MAKEUP: Avant Gard Hair Salon Team
PHOTO: Scott Bryant
Art Direction by Larry Oskin &
The Marketing
Solutions Team

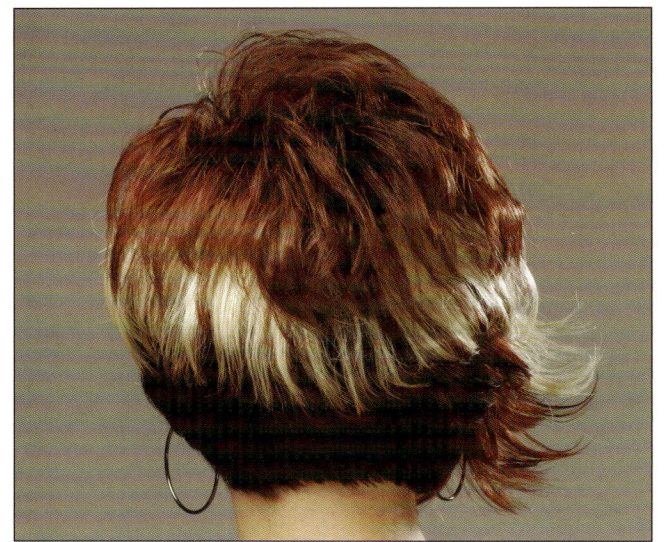

Indiana's Premier Hair Academy
HAIR: Josef Settle
COLOR: Josef Settle
MAKEUP: Indiana's Premier Hair Academy Team
PHOTO: Scott Bryant
Art Direction by Larry Oskin & Marketing Solutions Team

CREATIVE COLOR

Salon De Christé
HAIR: Andrea Shumate
MAKEUP: Molly Shipman
PHOTO: Heather Ramirez

élon Salon
HAIR: Kelley Newman
COLOR: Kelley Newman
MAKEUP: Kristin Harrell
PHOTO: Scott Bryant
Art Direction by Larry Oskin &
The Marketing Solutions Team

Infrashine
HAIR: Steve and Cyndi Lehman for InfraShine
MAKEUP: Jaime Queenin
PHOTO: Taggart Winterhalter for Purely Visual

HAIR: Angela Smith
MAKEUP: Mickey Guedea
PHOTO: Eliisa Maki

CREATIVE COLOR

PON International- Anaheim Hills, CA
HAIR: Morgan Jackson
MAKE-UP: Sara Wayne
PHOTO: Taggart Winterhalter for Purely Visual

Avant Gard Hair Salon
HAIR: A.J. Williams
COLOR: A.J. Williams
MAKEUP: Lacey Walker
PHOTO: Scott Bryant
Art Direction by Larry Oskin & The Marketing Solutions Team

Fresh A.H.S.
HAIR: Deborah Gavin
PHOTO: Babak
*Courtesy of NAHA

Index volume sixty seven

Salon	Photographer	Page
Achurra Designs	Steven Ledell	2
Advanced College of Cosmetology	Doug Raflik	40
Alexander's Grand Salon & Spa	Taggart Winterhalter for Purely Visual	30,31,34,62
Anazao Salon	Robert B. Pendley	8,63
Angela Smith	Eliisa Maki	63,94
Art of Hair Salon	Taggart Winterhalter for Purely Visual	43,49
Avant Gard Hair Salon	Scott Bryant	46,48,83,92,95
Beauty First	Amanda Knight	90
Blue Chair Salon	Blue Chair Salon	84
Brittany's Spa Salon	Scott Bryant	26
Carter T. Lund & Associates	Taggart Winterhalter for Purely Visual	5,36
CinderellaHair	Taggart Winterhalter for Purely Visual	55,58
Cosmos Hair and Day Spa	Taggart Winterhalter for Purely Visual	40
Creative Design A.T.C.	Brian Morgan	67
Créme Colour Lounge	Taggart Winterhalter for Purely Visual	17
Diadema Hair Fashion	Stefano Bidini	50
Doyle Designed Salon	Deborah Zaniolo	41
Edie's Styling Center	Scott Bryant	57,65,66,67
élon Salon	Scott Bryant	23,32,35,39,51,59,61,93
ENJOY Hair Care	Taggart Winterhalter for Purely Visual	22,24,33
Eveline Charles Salons & Spas	Darren Greenwood	28,87
Fantastic Sams, Brea, CA	Taggart Winterhalter for Purely Visual	68
Fantastic Sams, Carson, CA	Taggart Winterhalter for Purely Visual	28
Fantastic Sams, Corona, CA	Taggart Winterhalter for Purely Visual	42,85
Fantastic Sams, Corona, CA	Taggart Winterhalter for Purely Visual	78
Fantastic Sams, Lake Elsinore, CA	Taggart Winterhalter for Purely Visual	42
Fantastic Sams, Norco, CA	Taggart Winterhalter for Purely Visual	68
Fantastic Sams, San Dimas, CA	Taggart Winterhalter for Purely Visual	41
Fantastic Sams, Wildomar, CA	Taggart Winterhalter for Purely Visual	88
FilmMagic	Michael Tran	71
FilmMagic	Jason LaVeris	73
FilmMagic	Jon Kopaloff	74,75,76,77
FilmMagic	Michael Loccisano	76
FilmMagic	Jason Merritt	77
*Fresh A.H.S.	Babak	96
Getty Images	Amy Sussman	70
Getty Images	Frank Micelotta	70
Getty Images	Evan Agostini	72
Getty Images	Pascal Le Segretain	72
Getty Images	Michale Buckner	73
Getty Images	Peter Kramer	74
Getty Images	Byron Gamarro	75
Goldwell	Goldwell	79
Goldwell Colorance Team	Goldwell	60
Graham Webb International Academy of Hair	Scott Bryant	52
Hair Benders Internationalé	Scott Bryant	7,53
Indiana's Premier Hair Academy	Scott Bryant	89,92
Infrashine	Taggart Winterhalter for Purely Visual	9,21,27,54,94
Intercoiffure	Yannick	14
Intercoiffure Mondial	Romualdo Piore	64
John Amico Haircare & Jayld Haircolor	Scott Bryant	82
Kadus USA	Taggart Winterhalter for Purely Visual	11
Kathy Adams Salon	Tom Carson Photography	51,84
London Salon and Spa	Ed Flores	69
Michael Angelo Salon & Spa	Michael Razzo	4
Mina's Studio and Spa	Jan Balster	48
Mitchell's Salons & Day Spas	Annette McCall	47
Pivot Point International	Mike van den Toom/David Placek	80
Pivot Point International, Germany	Mike van den Toom/Tina Rayyan	86
Planet Salon	Jeff Rogers	8
PON International	Taggart Winterhalter for Purely Visual	16,29,44,45,56,95
Robert Allen Salon	Boyer Images LLC	81,91
Rubia Salon & Spa	Jim Laatsch	90
Salon De Christé	Heather Ramirez	93
Salon Dé Dawn	Taggart Winterhalter for Purely Visual	18,37
Salon Serene	Jean Sweet	15,25,26,38
Sempre Bellezza	Taggart Winterhalter for Purely Visual	13,20
Siggers Hairdressers Salon	Scott Bryant	6
Stray Cuts	Taggart Winterhalter for Purely Visual	20
Tangles Hair Lounge	Taggart Winterhalter for Purely Visual	19
Vincent Michael Salon	Taggart Winterhalter for Purely Visual	3,10,12,19
WireImage	Anthony Harvey	70
WireImage	Jean-Paul Aussenard	70
WireImage	Kmazur	72,73,75
WireImage	Gregg DeGuire	73
WireImage	Barry King	74
WireImage	Nick Harvey	74
WireImage	Steve Granitz	75
WireImage	Eamonn McCormack	76
WireImage	Jeffery Mayer	77

*Courtesy of NAHA-North American Hairstyling Awards